ASIAN ALLURE

A compilation of inspirational creations
from prominent Asian designers

Wildflower Media
PO Box 4368
Topeka, KS 66604

Copywriter: Marti Boone CFD
Copy Editors: David Coake, Cres Motzi AIFD EMC

Art Director: Kathleen Dillinger
Graphic Designer: Nicole Liu

President and Publisher: Travis Rigby
Managing Director: Jane DeMarco

Printed in China

ISBN 978-0-9854743-5-5
First Edition

CONTENTS

FORWARD
by Leanne + David Kesler AIFD PFCI FDI

What a wonderfully creative book. We are delighted to see this compilation of floral art come to fruition. Jeanne Ha, Greg Lum and Lily Chan have succeeded in creating a beautiful treasury of inspiring floral designs by 14 accomplished Asian designers. From simple linear designs and intricate handiwork of flowers-to-wear to large, dramatic, and complex contemporary displays, beautiful flowers are the soul of this book.

Organized by the tactile inspirations of wood, fabric, paper and metal, each design is a distinctive work of art showcased by marvelous photography. *Asian Allure*, a compilation of inspirational designs is a must-have for the library of every serious floral designer. A true work of love, this book calls for a heartfelt thank-you to all of the designers sharing their talents.

Leanne Kesler AIFD PFCI FDI
David Kesler AIFD PFCI FDI
Floral Design Institute

Newly into my role as publisher of *Florists' Review* magazine, I was approached by Jeanne Ha, Greg Lum and Lily Chan with a book concept that both celebrates and expands our ideas of Asian-inspired floral design. It was hard to resist the knowledge and passion of these three Asian floral powerhouses, and so we embarked on our first collaboration with specific designers to create an amazing design book.

We couldn't be more thrilled with the outcome. I'm sure you will agree that the result is boldly inspiring. Thanks to Jeanne, Greg and Lily, as well as the awesome array of designers they engaged to participate, we have cutting-edge floral design to encourage our own personal design styles or simply beautify our coffee and bedside tables.

Enjoy!

Travis Rigby
Publisher of *Wildflower Media*
Florists' Review and Super Floral magazines

ABOUT THE
ARTISTS

Greg Lum AIFD EMC

Greg Lum hopes the floral designs in this book will inspire people to try new types of designs and to learn to discover their own unique styles. This volume is a compilation of works by prominent Asian designers, showcasing their distinctive design aesthetics.

"I enjoy sharing design ideas and experiences with others so that they may be inspired to create something fresh and exciting, to be the best designers they can be. It is what makes our industry thrive and grow, by educating each other and sharing our life experiences," Lum said.

After earning his Bachelor of Science degree in Environmental Horticultural Science from California Polytechnic State University, San Luis Obispo, Lum went on to continue his studies in Retail Floristry / Ornamental Horticulture at City College of San Francisco. Today, he finds sources of creativity and inspiration from pieces of art, nature, a container or plant materials, other designers and his Chinese culture.

With his participation in numerous design competitions over the past 20 years, Greg Lum has earned an impressive reputation by winning many prestigious awards. When asked what his dream project would be, Lum answered, "To be one of the judges for the Tournament of Roses Parade."

In addition to this book, some of the many publications Greg Lum has been featured in are *Fleur Creatif*, *Signature Weddings Asia*, *Flowers in Love 3*, *Flowers LIBETbl*, *LIBETbl World*, *Clip … Flores y Mas*, *Floriology*, *Floral Monthly*, *Flowers&* and *Florists' Review*.

Jeanne Ha AIFD

Jeanne Ha was born and raised in Seoul, South Korea, and grew up learning Ikebana design from her mother. "I have better understandings of how early spring blooming branches cast their shadow on the traditional Korean house roof or how an Ikebana design can be best displayed on a simple wood stand. Or how such bright, almost cheesy, Chinese silk can be shown beautifully."

After getting married, she moved to Washington, DC; however, all the memories of her childhood are still beautifully painted and stored in her mind. With this book, Ha wanted to share her ideas with fellow florists and future florists. She is inspired by the "Asian flair" exhibited by designers of Asian heritage, and showcasing the standout work of these floral artists is the basis for this book.

After earning a Bachelor of Arts degree in Voice and Master of Arts degree in Musicology from Seoul National University, Ha went on to study Excellence in Design at the Benz School of Floral Design in Austin, Texas. She has participated in numerous design competitions, served on several committees and opened a shop, Park Florist, in Takoma Park, Md., in 2004.

Lily Chan AIFD EMC

Lily Chan believes we are all here for a reason: "A life journey to experience as much as we can," adding, "We are all born to do what we choose to do; whether we take it or not, it is our choice." It is with this choice in mind that Chan approached this book – to share some of her ideas that can be easily translated to being spiritual and quiet.

Chan looks to sharing and giving back to the floral industry, from which she derives inspiration, as well as from nature and unique buildings and structures. "I find my inspirations from nature. Most of the time, I look toward the horizon or the skyline, with its new structures in the background. All the older buildings, with their unique structures from the 1850s to the present, are amazing. Going to museums, gallery openings, even the theater are all inspirational; however, most of all, my colleagues in the floral industry inspire me with their designs – whether it be a program, workshop or just working alongside them."

Following her education at the City College of San Francisco, Chan participated in numerous design competitions and has been a member of the California State Floral Association for many years. She has also been a featured designer in several design programs, exhibited at shows and festivals, held office as a board member and association judge, and was featured in the *Nob Hill Gazette* prior to the publication of *Asian Allure*.

WOOD

When we think of design elements that inspire us, wood is the first one to come to mind. Wood is one of the most familiar elements we can use in design. It is an element that has endless possibilities, and as we created floral designs with various sticks, branches and bark, we emphasized our familiarity and comfort with the element and explored a range of emotions. Some of the designers used wood elements to create a modern and chic style, some created a rustic feel and others used wood as a focal emphasis.

| Greg Lum AIFD EMC

East meets West, and that fusion influences this free-form design that celebrates the timeless yin-and-yang relationship between wood and floral materials, as *Chrysanthemum x morifolium* provides a canopy of golden-yellows over *Tillandsia usneoides* varieties 'Super Fine Gray' and 'Kimberly' and weathered driftwood.

Jeanne Ha AIFD

A parallel design is anchored by exotic *Dicranopteris linearis* coils and *Philodendron* 'Xanadu'. Negative space between the prominent lines draws the eyes downward to the ghost wood and interlocked groupings of *Anthurium andreanum*, *Leucadendron* spp., *Jasminum polyanthum*, *Cordyline terminalis*, *Berzelia abrotanoides* and *Colmanara* Wildcat 'Lorraine'. The result is dark and masculine.

MATERIALS: *Dicranopteris linearis*, *Philodendron* 'Xanadu', *Anthurium andreanum*, *Leucadendron* spp., *Jasminum polyanthum*, *Cordyline terminalis*, *Berzelia abrotanoides*, *Colmanara* Wildcat 'Lorraine'

Large vertical ghost-wood pieces with interlaced *Linum usitatissimum* create contrast and contemplation; pale versus bright, rippled versus smooth, fresh versus dried. Bulky wood elements create composition dominance with movement in numerous directions by *Aechmea chantinii*, *Phormium tenax*, *Cymbidium* spp., *Anthurium andreanum*, *Cordyline fruticosa* and *Aloe striatula*.

This modern-day hand-held bouquet features a minimal color palette with rich textures and cascading downward movement. White and ivory-hued *Chrysanthemum x morifolium* and *Ranunculus asiaticus* command attention and draw the eyes further down to *Philodendron* 'Xanadu', *Zantedeschia aethiopica* and *Rhipsalis cassutha* against suspended gravity-defying pieces of ghost wood.

Greg Lum AIFD EMC

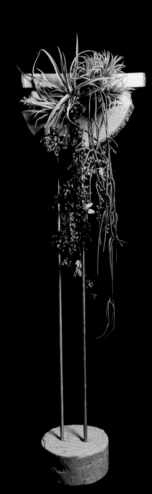

Inspired by a passion for fusing natural with unnatural elements and materials, Greg utilizes a cement base with threaded metal rods to support a standing design of permanent *Tillandsia harrissi*, *Tillandsia ionantha*, *Colmanara* Wildcat 'Lorraine', *Senecio rowleyanus* and *Rhipsalis cassutha*.

A wreath of *Betula* spp. bark supports the weight of numerous overlapping reddish-orange *Zantedeschia aethiopica* in a design that signals the seasonal transition from fall to winter. Heavily arching *Zantedeschia* heads bow to the cold like a traditional East Asian welcome to the first frost created by white wax shavings encircling the composition.

Lily Chan AIFD EMC

Inspired by Asian and European influences,
this simple design incorporates *Morus alba*
branches rising upward in a gentle gesture
to conceal glass water tubes, as well as to
guide the viewers' eyes to delicate *Lathyrus
odoratus* blooms that seem to stand unpicked.

Tall vertical lines of multiple
red-brown *Cornus alba* branches,
native to Korea and Northern
China, are wired one by one to
create a standing structure.
Key to the overall design aesthetic
is the ascending movement and
warm color palette where papery
headed white and orange *Papaver
nudicaule* appear wild and new.

Yukari Mitsui AIFD EMC |

Demonstrating a passion and respect for the majesty of Mother Nature is a large and unassuming piece of driftwood, which serves as the backdrop and design foundation for a vertical composition of *Moluccella laevis*, *Ornithogalum arabicum*, *Pandanus baptistii*, *Phalaenopsis* spp. and *Philodendron* 'Xanadu'.

Photo by Antonio Lopez Photography

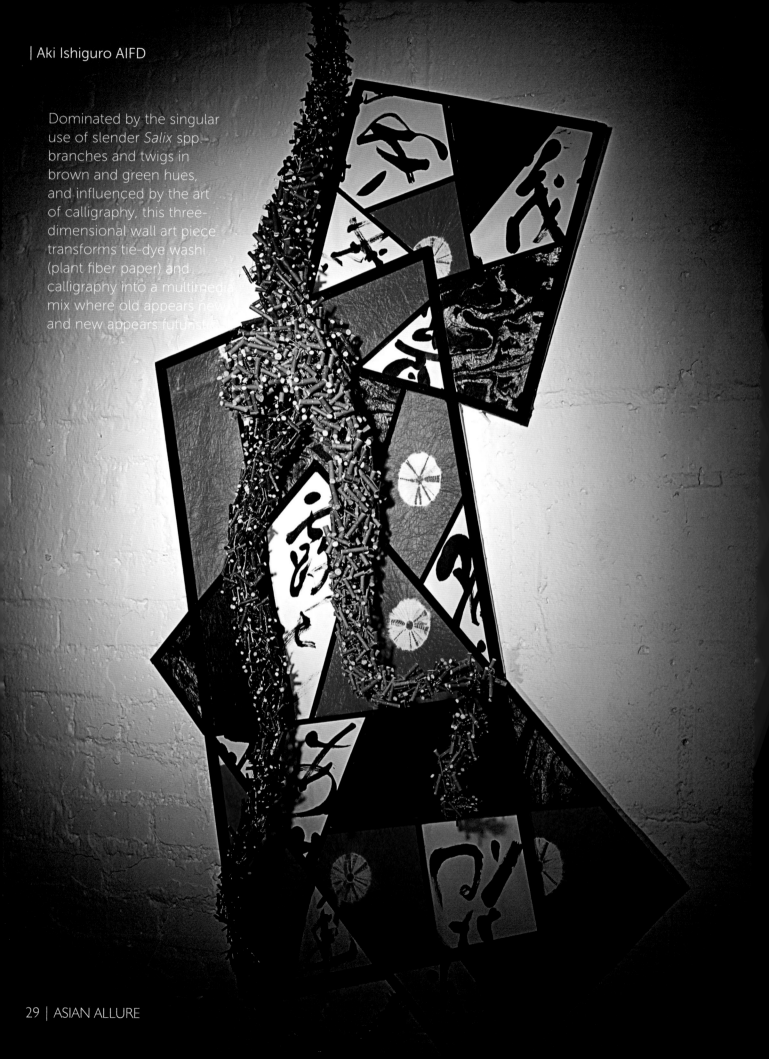

| Aki Ishiguro AIFD

Dominated by the singular use of slender *Salix* spp. branches and twigs in brown and green hues, and influenced by the art of calligraphy, this three-dimensional wall art piece transforms tie-dye washi (plant fiber paper) and calligraphy into a multimedia mix where old appears new and new appears futuristic.

An armature constructed of wired *Cornus alba* branches provide an airy framework for golden *Cymbidium* spp. blooms and red-brown *Graptopetalum* spp. rosettes, with design inspiration derived from a strong sense of color and lifelong exploration of analogous and complementary color combinations.

Wood and minimal flower choices echo a happy Asian childhood that instilled frugality and appreciation for simple abundance as seen in these two wood compositions where both designs achieve the concept "less is more." The composition is inspired by all that Mother Nature provides, including newly pruned tree branches. Materials include *Acer negundo*, *Skimmia japonica* and *Liriope muscari*.

| Louisa Lam AIFD PFCI CPFD

An original reverent homage to Asian cultural celebrations of nature, this "living sculpture" is designed to showcase the power of nature. The colors and textures of *Helleborus* spp., *Chamelaucium* spp. and *Ruscus hypoglossum* seem to thrive on a piece of floating driftwood.

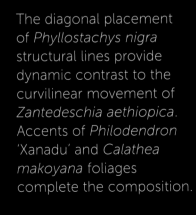

The diagonal placement of *Phyllostachys nigra* structural lines provide dynamic contrast to the curvilinear movement of *Zantedeschia aethiopica*. Accents of *Philodendron* 'Xanadu' and *Calathea makoyana* foliages complete the composition.

Joy, derived from the design journey and creative process, springs to life a modern-day secret garden composition that is abundant with *Conium maculatum, Eucalyptus* spp., *Dianthus caryophyllus, Alstroemeria* spp. 'Primadonna', *Chrysanthemum x morifolium, Tulipa* spp., *Mokara (Vanda x Ascocentrum x Arachnis), Cupressus* spp., *Nephrolepis cordifolia, Aeonium haworthii, Rosa* spp. 'Santa Barbara', *Crocosmia aurea* and *Lolium multiflorum.*

FABRIC

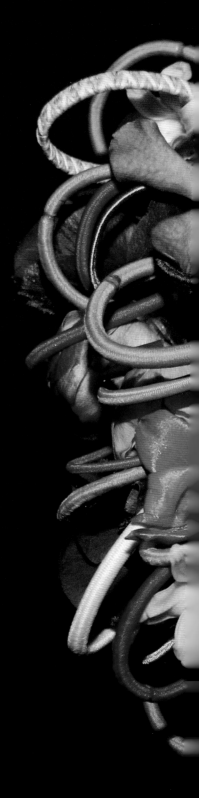

When creating floral designs with the addition of fabric, we exposed not only to textiles used in clothing but also yarns, ribbons, handcrafted felt, jute, wool, tapestry and weavings. As designers we can incorporate new textures into our floral compositions by adding fabric elements. While ribbon is commonly used, there is a wealth of other textiles, derived from both plants and animals, that can add textural diversity, unachievable with floral materials alone, to a living work of art.

| Toni Tibbits AIFD

A visual explosion of spirited and electrifying colors and textures highlight the intrinsic relationship between everyday fabrics and floral possibilities. Applications of interlaced *Ornithogalum dubium*, *Phalaenopsis* spp., *Ranunculus asiaticus*, *Anemone coronaria* and *Helleborus* spp. appear fluid with movement.

Ranunculus asiaticus is the inspiration for this composition's blend of blush pink and coral hues. Gradations of pink and peach tonal values of *Gerbera jamesonii*, *Tulipa* spp., *Ranunculus asiaticus*, *Phalaenopsis* spp. and *Jasminum polyanthum* are contrasted by neutral gray wired felt and knitted cords atop a large bowl.

A sublime marriage between past and present takes place in a bridal bouquet complemented by a traditional Asian fabric-wrapped collar. The design is elevated by precise groupings of *Rosa* spp. 'Freedom', *Anthurium andraeanum*, *Ranunculus asiaticus*, *Fatsia japonica*, *Cordyline fruticosa* and *Senecio rowleyanus*.

| Jeanne Ha AIFD

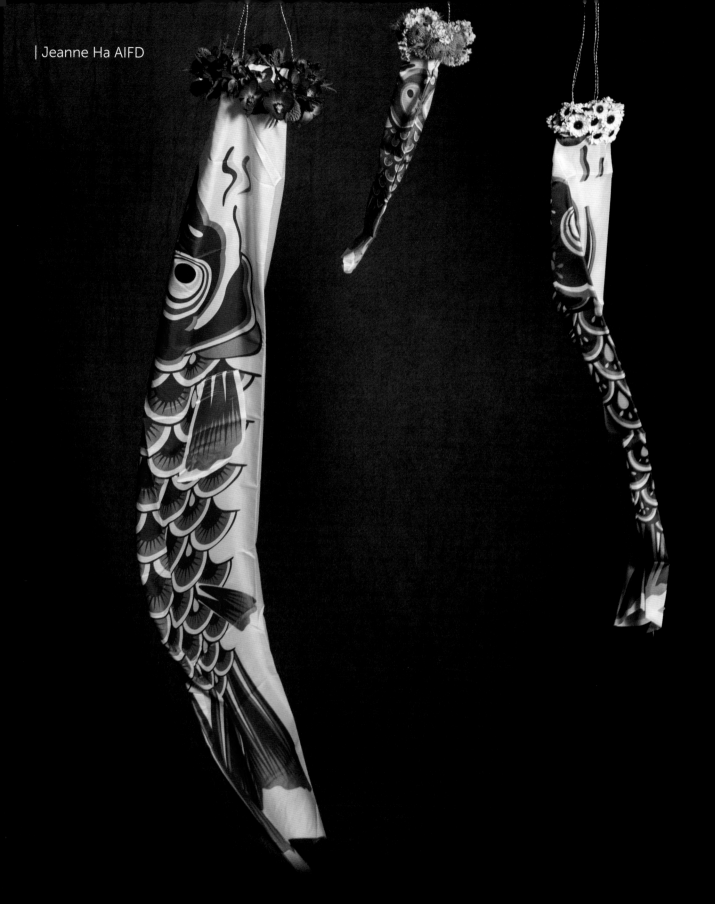

Inspired by Japan's annual Children's Day celebration and the designer's own children, floral elements are added to "koinobori" carp-shaped windsocks, including *Delphinium elatum*, *Viburnum opulus* 'Roseum', *Chrysanthemum x morifolium*, *Dianthus barbatus* 'Green Trick' and *Eryngium planum*.

| Greg Lum AIFD EMC

The ultimate unconventional Valentine's Day design, this trio of white vases boasts heart-shaped *Anthurium andraeanum* and wildly spiraling *Allium sphaerocephalon* arising from a textural bases of sisal *(Agave sisalana)* hearts, small balls and trails of pink wool. Communicating "I'm crazy about you" or "My funny Valentine" looks like this!

An exquisite antique *"obi"* (Japanese kimono sash) forms a coiled satin base for an inspired contemporary design where *Hypericum androsaemum, Helleborus* spp., *Astilbe arendsii, Liriope muscari* and *Kalanchoe* spp. emerge from its folds to carry forward the fabric patterns and color palette while negative space in the center mimics interior petals poised to open and bloom.

This elaborate bouquet is composed of *Arctostaphylos* spp. branches that are wired together with a twig garland and finished with a wool-covered handle. *Guzmania lingulata*, *Celosia cristata*, *Rhipsalis teres*, *Gerbera jamesonii*, *Aeonium haworthii* and *Ascocenda (Ascocentrum x Vanda)* are glued in and appear to move up and down the armature in a color-coordinated fashion. An overlay of a fruited *Diplocyclos palmatus* vine adds movement and interest.

Reminiscent of colorful Japanese kimonos billowing in the wind, hundreds of one-inch square plastic boards wrapped in fabric are placed at varying levels to create an uneven surface before arranging *Chrysanthemum x morifolium*, *Dahlia pinnata*, *Hydrangea macrophylla* and *Celosia cristata* against an implied mosaic sheath. The golden *Arctostaphylos* spp. branch accent elevates its refinement and importance.

Photo: MJ Cardenas

A nest-like shape of felt tiles and dried *Gossypium arboreum* invokes a surreal and safe – yet highly unusual – habitat for *Paphiopedilum* spp. and *Liriope muscari* to appear like futuristic life forms.

In a composition influenced by the fragility of nature and its vulnerability to mankind, the power of texture imparts a distinct sense of peril as *Echinacea angustifolia*, *Anigozanthos flavidus* and *Trachelium caeruleum* cascade down from a wool wrapped earth-like sphere on a formidable branch of *Poncirus trifoliata*.

Repetition of the distinctive shapes of *Lagenaria siceraria*, with added repetition of textural accents, lend stark contrast for emphasis on the solitary placement of a deep red *Anthurium andraeanum*.

| Louisa Lam AIFD PFCI CPFD

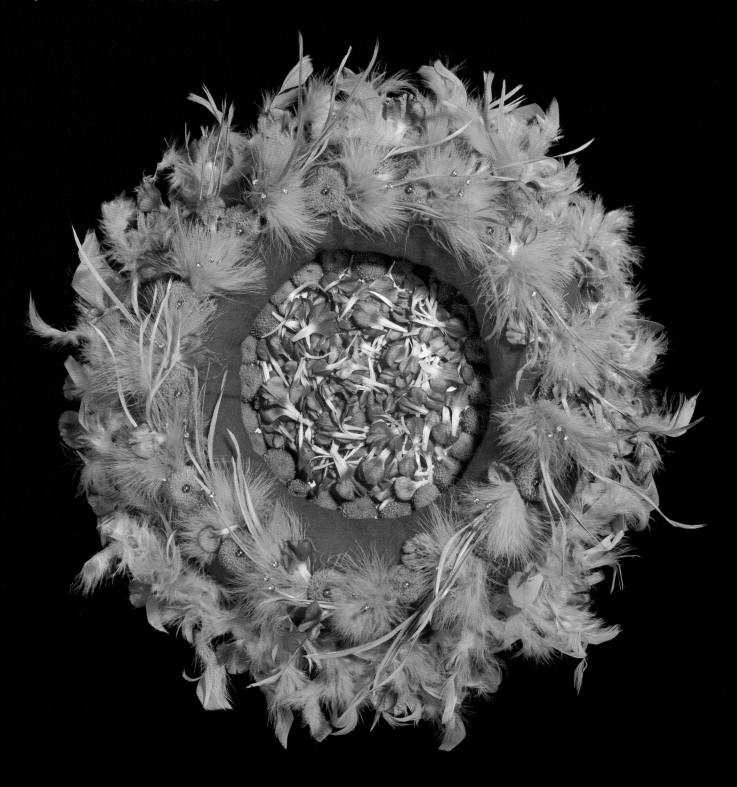

Key elements are deconstructed and rearranged into circles according to their nature, color and texture, to create different aesthetics from multiple angles. Repetition of shape and movement of *Chrysanthemum x morifolium* blooms and *Dianthus caryophyllus* petals further communicate the importance of a circle's symbolic meanings of completeness and perfection in Asian cultures.

With inspiration from wrapping wool onto wire to create a wearable design, this wearable art design is fashioned from *Eucalyptus* spp., *Scabiosa* spp., *Berzelia lanuginosa* and rattan/ Midollino sticks (*Calamus* spp.).

PAPER

As we explore our culture, we pay close attention to the importance of paper. Paper is much more than an empty canvas on which to write or draw. Korean rice paper (hanji), Chinese paper fans, paper lanterns and Japanese origami papers illustrate just a few examples of the ways in which paper has become an Asian cultural symbol. Easily incorporated into floral designs, paper can inspire and enable designers to be more creative, and they can impart a transparent look or add feelings of lightness or excitement with patterns and colors.

| Louisa Lam AIFD PFCI CPFD

The paper fan sometimes represents peace and harmony for the world, and in doing so, it can be used with botanical materials to extend a symbolic narrative to express hopes and new beginnings.

White Chinese paper fans hang in the air on bamboo sticks with celestial lightness and a monochromatic color scheme, lending emphasis to texture and shape. The design is anchored with *Rosa* spp. and *Gloriosa* spp., but other botanicals include *Dianthus barbatus* 'Green Trick', *Berzelia albiflora*, *Freesia* spp., *Craspedia globosa*, *Mokara* (*Arachnis* x *Ascocentrum* x *Vanda*), *Cytisus scoparius* and *Allium sphaerocephalon*.

This geometric design takes shape in custom-made hexagonal white cardboard structures with permanent botanicals of *Phalaenopsis* spp., *Echeveria* spp. and *Senecio rowleyanus*.

Shredded paper sphere topped with *Phalaenopsis* spp.

This multilayered suspension bouquet blends Ikebana simplicity with progressive and stylistic design freedoms. *Lirope muscari* leaves are woven and framed with a collage of origami papers that contrast pristine *Phalaenopsis* spp. blooms and *Hypericum androsaemum* berries.

This interpretive design is
created with two inverted
teardrop cardboard shapes
trimmed and covered with
rice paper to create an "eye"
silhouette. Deconstructed
Dianthus caryophyllus petals are
affixed to achieve texture in the
completed composition.

Classic Asian floral-motif fabric frames an unexpected shadow-box design replete with *Liriope gigantea*, *Calathea lancifolia*, *Aspidistra elatior* and *Xerophyllum tenax*. The repetitive use of monochromatic lime and dark greens, strong linear and curvilinear movements, and contrasting textures creates a pleasing rhythm

A less-is-more aesthetic is realized when *Phalaenopsis* spp. and *Vaccinium* spp. are balanced above a repurposed paperback book. Minimalism design lends the viewers' eyes a place to rest, contemplate and experience a sense of ease within.

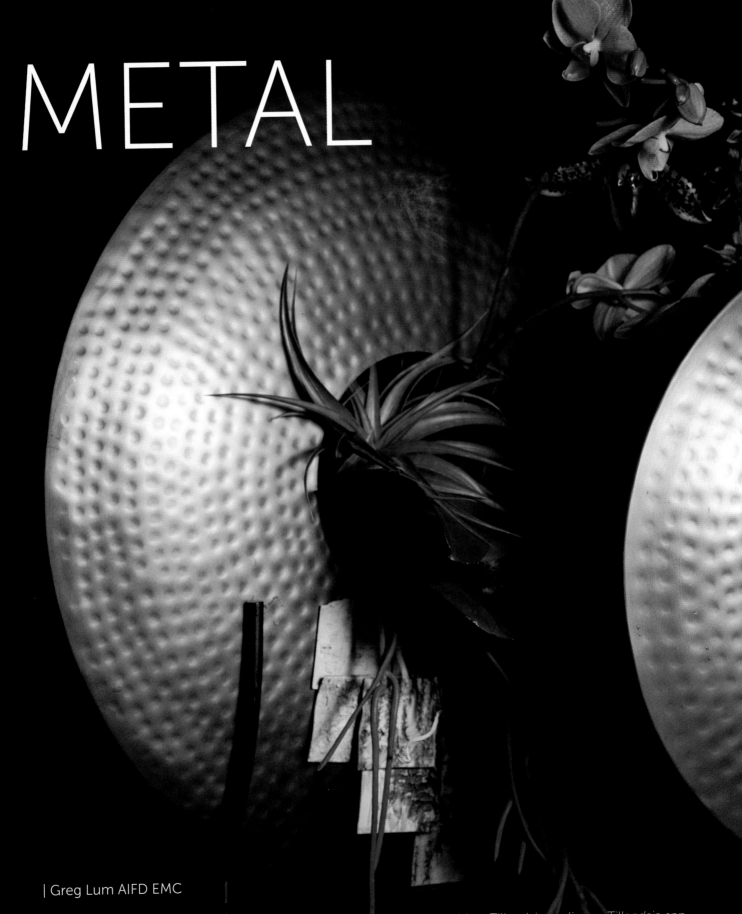

METAL

| Greg Lum AIFD EMC

MATERIALS: *Euphorbia medusa, Rhipsalis cassutha, Tillandsia xerographica, Tillandsia scaligera, Tillandsia* spp., *Phalaenopsis* spp., *Paphiopedilum* spp., *Colmanara* Wildcat 'Lorraine', *Betula* spp.

When used in floral designs, metal can be a reflective source, in contrast to the textures of the natural botanicals. To some, metal can be cold, heavy and solid, but to a floral designer, it can provoke emotion and creativity.

| Greg Lum AIFD EMC

This trio of unique and complex designs
makes use of metal trash cans as vessels
that are topped with plastic-foam wreath
forms covered with foam packing material
(bean-bag peanuts), each of which is
attached to the wreath form with a pearl-
headed corsage pin. The crumpled paper in
and around the design is intended to add a
touch of humor, referencing office garbage
mixed with an intricate floral design.
Botanical materials include *Rosa* spp.
'Avalanche' and *Tillandsia xerographica*.

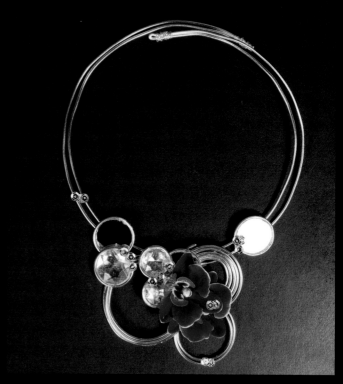

MATERIALS: Aluminum wire, bullion wire, *Craspedia globosa*, *Freesia* spp., *Mokara (Arachnis x Ascocentrum x Vanda)*

MATERIALS: Aluminum wire, mirror disks, *Cymbidium* spp.

MATERIALS: Aluminum wire, flat wire, *Chamelaucium uncinatum*, *Narcissus cyclamineus*, *Ranunculus asiaticus*

MATERIAL: *Colmanara* Wildcat 'Lorraine'

Floral jewelry adds natural and couture-worthy dimension to ladies' and men's outerwear with real, innovative and highly-stylized options. Various orchid combinations around the neckline of a little black dress or cascading down a man's tuxedo lapel rival static two-dimensional jewelry, thanks to color, texture, fragrance and one-of-a-kind design inspirations.

Art imitates life in this composition that teases the eyes as the spiky flowers of *Strelitzia reginae* repeat the form of the container. The vibrant, iridescent orange petals juxtaposed with the dark metal strengthens the impact. The color and texture of *Craspedia globosa* and *Dianthus barbatus* 'Green Trick' provide additional color, form and texture to this free-form design.

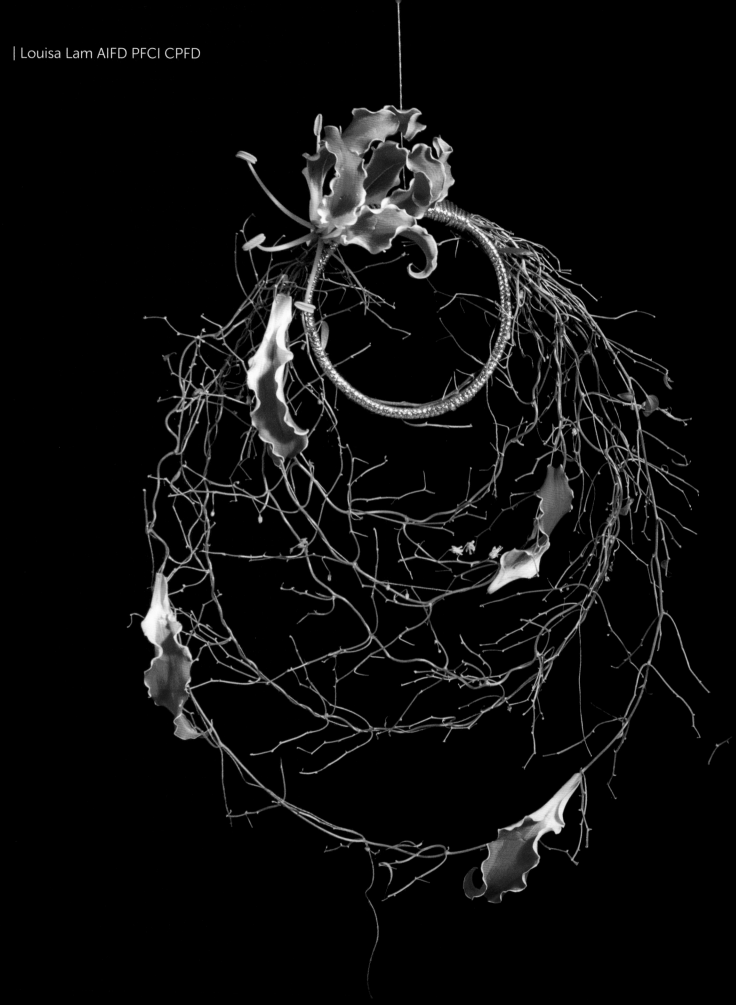

These two hanging creations are intended as a singular arrangement. Although the materials in each composition are different, repetition and rhythm occur in the graduated loops (metallic wire in one, deciduous *Vaccinium* spp. in the other) and the banding on the smallest loops. Other botanicals include *Gloriosa rothschildiana* and *Asparagus asparagoides*.

Paying homage to Japanese festivals
like *Tsukimi*, *Otsukimi* or *Jugoya*
that honor the autumn moon,
this, too, is a celebration of design
interpretations that are influenced
by mankind's deep connection
to nature. *Miscanthus sinensis*,
Setaria italica, *Chrysanthemum x
morifolium*, *Phytolacca americana*,
Gomphrena globosa and *Celosia
cristata* come together to evoke
emotional responses that focus on
autumn. Additional elements come
into play depending on the time of
day and shadows each flower and
paper bird create.

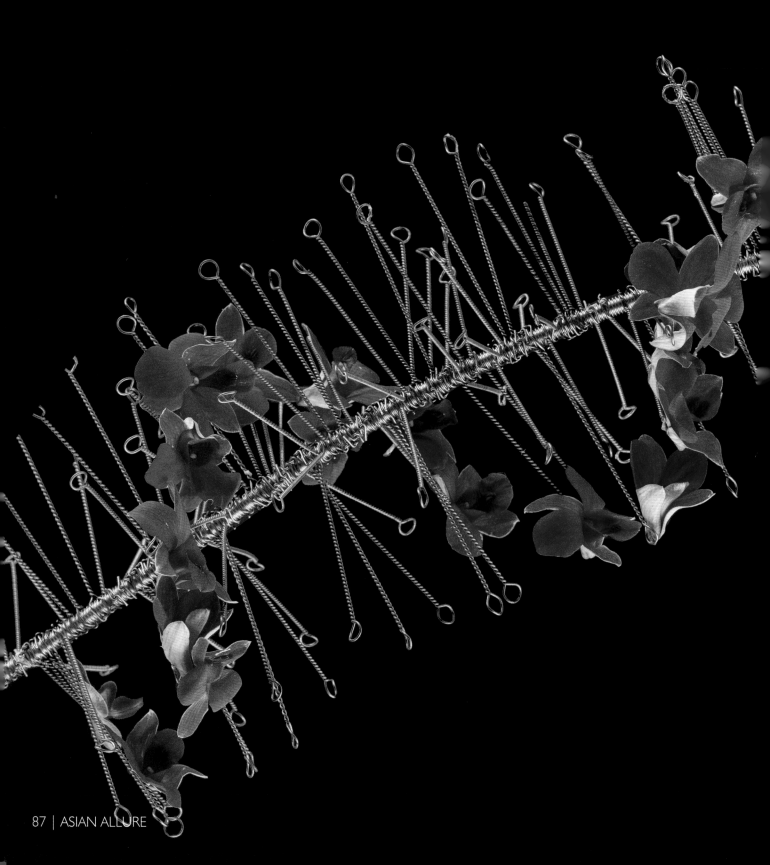

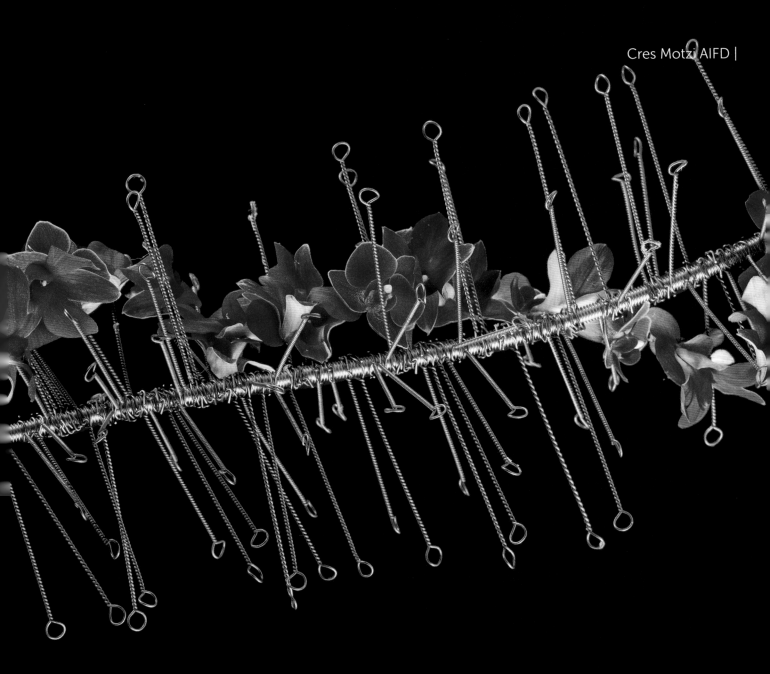

A five-foot-long piece of is shaped into a graceful curve and welded onto a metal plate for stability. Heavy-duty ties are fastened with a wire twister to the threads on the rebar, to keep the ties from slipping. *Dendrobium* spp. blooms are glued in an elongated zigzag fashion to accentuate the curve of the rebar.

Exuding a "think outside the box" mentality, this unique composition combines an unlikely pairing of *Phalaenopsis* spp. and *Rubus idaeus* in a dark, menacing and industrial metal pin vessel.

Rusty and reimagined wine barrel bands are secured with wired twigs to create an outward framework for a microcosm of new plant life. *Echinocystis lobata, Aptenia cordifolia* 'Red Apple', *Aeonium haworthii, Crassula ovata, Scabiosa atropurpurea* pods, *Tropaeolum majus* leaves, *Tradescantia* spp., dried *Banksia* spp. foliage, *Cupressus sempervirens, Hypsizygus tessellatus, Agave* spp. leaf, *Buddleia* spp. branches and *Avena fatua*, all thrive in an unconventional setting.

This book is about working together and bringing our unique styles of design to you! We hope that you will be inspired by the designs we present. It is our wish that by sharing our knowledge, others can learn and grow and become better designers. Mutual sharing and learning is the only way that our industry can thrive and grow.

This is a labor of love with a compilation of works by wonderful artists who have become forever friends in life. Through excellent teamwork ethics and determination, this project came to fruition.

Ikuko Hashimoto AIFD

Ikuko Hashimoto has a passion for Japanese floral design and is adept at incorporating its principles into traditional American floral design. As a native of Japan, she grew up with Ikebana. After moving to New York in 1990, she worked as a freelance designer for 10 years. Ikuko was inducted into the American Institute of Floral Designers (AIFD) in 2005 and became an AIFD Certified Floral Evaluator/Judge in 2013. She is currently the lead designer at Brady's Floral in the Phoenician Resort in Scottsdale, Arizona.

Yukari Mitsui AIFD EMC

Yukari Mitsui is an award-winning designer at Unique Floral Design & Events and a lead designer at Bloomstar, Canada's largest fresh flower importer and ready-made bouquet provider for mass-market retailers. She was inducted into the American Institute of Floral Designers (AIFD) in 2009, and then recognized as an AIFD Certified Floral Evaluator/Judge in 2015. She has also successfully completed the European Master Certification (EMC) program in 2012.

Aki Ishiguro AIFD

Aki Ishiguro is a freelance floral designer who specializes in unique personal flowers and arrangements. She learned the basic techniques of floral design while studying at Keisen Women Junior College Horticulture Department in Kanagawa, Japan. She continued her studies at the Roppongi Keisen Flower Design School and took the instructor qualification. In 1994, she received a bachelor's degree in horticulture at Mississippi State University. She was inducted into the American Institute of Floral Designers (AIFD) in 2017.

Brenna Quan AIFD

Brenna Quan's foundation as an artist began with the study of lines and movement as a young dancer, which led to her transition into the art of floral design. As she matured, she gained extensive experience in retail floristry, including wedding and event design. She has won multiple awards in local and international floral design competitions and has been a featured design-er on the AIFD National Symposium stage, at the Ninth Moon Floral Design Showcase and for local Floral Art Club events. Making her home in Vancouver, BC, Canada, Brenna was inducted into the American Institute of Floral Designers (AIFD) in 2009.

Kiyomi Kurihara AIFD

Kiyomi Kurihara is a floral designer and certified Ikebana teacher known for working diligently with great attention to detail in her work. She started her career as a floral designer while living in Dallas, Texas, and was inducted into AIFD in 2015. She currently lives in Nagasaki, Japan, where World Flower Show at Huis Ten Bosch is held annually. In addition to Ikebana-influenced designs, she is also skilled in American, European, modern and classic design. Her goal is to become a connection for great and detailed flower growers in Japan, as well as floral designers all over the world.

Susanne Law AIFD EMC

Susanne Law is a passionate educator, floral artist and student of the arts. She was inducted into the American Institute of Floral Designers (AIFD) in 2008 and completed the European Master Certification (EMC) program in 2012. Susanne has been an assistant to Tomas De Bruyne, Gregor Lersch and Per Benjamin and has assisted Hitomi Gilliam on numerous projects. She helped Hitomi develop the school curriculum and has taught for Design 358. She also taught for Adult Continuing Education Department at Surrey College for five years. For the past 19 years, Susanne has worked as one of the lead designers for La Belle Fleur Floral Boutique in Surrey, BC, Canada. She enjoys challenging herself with competitions while demonstrations allow her to continue teaching and sharing her passion with others.

Louisa Lam AIFD PFCI CPFD

Louisa Lam is an educator, award-winning floral artist, event consultant, newspaper columnist and TV show guest. She was the first Asian florist to obtain membership in the Canadian Professional Floral Designers Association (CPFDA) in 1991, and she was inducted into the American Institute of Floral Designers (AIFD) in 2009. Since being recognized as an AIFD Certified Floral Evaluator/Judge in 2013, Louisa has been involved in the Professional Floral Design Evaluation process from 2014 to 2017, as well as the Gateway to America's Cup Floral Design Competition from 2016 to 2017.

Louisa has been the head instructor and curriculum designer of the Professional Floral Art Diploma Program for the Vancouver School Board of Education since 1993. In 2014, she became the head instructor of the Professional Floral Art Diploma Program at Langara College in Vancouver, BC, Canada.

In 2017, Louisa was invited by AIFD to be a presenter at its National Symposium. Currently, in 2018, Louisa is the president of the Northwest Chapter of AIFD, vice chair of the AIFD National Membership Committee, and past chair of AIFD International Committee.

Gerard Toh AIFD

Gerard Toh is passionate about flowers and sharing his love of design. When he started competing, he won the California State Designer of the Year, which led him to become active in the floral community, participating in associations like the California State Floral Association, Teleflora's Los Angeles Coastal Counties Unit and becoming director-at-large of AIFD. He has been featured twice at AIFD's National Symposium and was chosen as the designer for an AIFD symposium gala dinner. Currently, he is focused on teaching and authoring books, as well as working as a design/marketing consultant with

Katherine Zhang is a passionate floral artist who was inducted into the American Institute of Floral Designers (AIFD) in 2006 and has competed in several prestigious design competitions. In 2007, she won the California State Floral Association's Top 10 Competition and became the State Designer of the Year. She has presented design programs at venues such as The Lan Su Chinese Garden for the Ninth Moon Floral Design Showcase, City College of San Francisco, Kitayama Brothers and Floral Artists of the Bay Area. She has served on the AIFD Northwest Chapter board of directors, and she has exhibited her work in and around the San Francisco Bay Area at places such as the annual Bouquets to Art and AIFD National Symposium.

Cres Motzi AIFD EMC

Cres Motzi is an internationally trained floral designer and educator whose studies have taken her to Belgium, France, Germany and Holland. She graduated from Boerma Instituut in Holland with diplomas in professional and advanced Dutch design in 2006, and she completed the European Master Certification (EMC) program in 2012. Cres was an inductee and a featured designer at the American Institute of Floral Designers' (AIFD) National Symposium in July 2010 and has participated with AIFD in the Philadelphia Flower Show since 2010, acting as chairman of the exhibit in 2017.

Cres has written tutorials and articles for *By Design*, a quarterly publication of the Garden Club of America. Her works have been published in *Flower Arranging the American Way* and *International Floral Art 2010-11* as well as the 2014-15 Jubilee editions. Cres is an AIFD Certified Floral Evaluator/Judge who is currently a freelance floral designer, demonstrator and an instructor at Longwood Gardens.

Toni Tibbits AIFD

Toni Tibbits founded Capri Floral & Event Design in Seattle, Washington, and has produced many large-scale and world-class events throughout the United States and Europe. In 2003, she was inducted into the American Institute of Floral Designers (AIFD) and since then has served on the AIFD Northwest Chapter board as vice president and treasurer. Toni has traveled extensively, where she has both competed in and judged many floral design competitions, including installations at Fleuramour in Belgium. She has been named one of the Top Ten Designers of the Year in California in 2009 and 2013, along with placing third in the Pacific Northwest Design Competition in 2018.

Photographers

TANYA CONSTANTINE
tanyaconstantine.com

COLIN GILLIAM
colingilliamphoto.com

BIANCA MADANAT
pixelbeephotography.com

Acknowledgements

Travis Rigby - *Florists' Review* and *Super Floral*   floristsreview.com; superfloral.com

Tanya Constantine - Tanya Constantine Photography   tanyaconstantine.com

Nancy Hayes - Nancy Hayes Casting   hayescasting.com

Brannan Street Wholesale Florist   brannanst.com

Gerry Gregg AIFD and Carol Gregg - Orange Man   orangemangerry@gmail.com

Leanne and David Kesler AIFD PFCI FDI - Floral Design Institute   flowerschool.com

Eric Tanouye - Green Point Nurseries   greenpointnursery.com

Colin Gilliam - Design 358   design358.com; colingilliamphoto.com

Bianca Madanat - Pixel Bee Photography   pixelbeephotography.com

Lieven Hemschoote - Fleur Creatif Magazine   www.fleurcreatif.com